# Monarchs

## and Other Butterflies

Book Author: Rob Knight
**For World Book:**
Editorial: Paul A. Kobasa, Maureen Liebenson, Christine Sullivan
Research: Andy Roberts, Loranne Shields
Graphics and Design: Melanie Bender, Sandra Dyrlund
Photos: Tom Evans, Sylvia Ohlrich
Permissions: Janet Peterson
Indexing: David Pofelski
Proofreading: Anne Dillon
Pre-press and Manufacturing: Carma Fazio, Anne Fritzinger, Steve Hueppchen, Madelyn Underwood

**For information about other World Book publications, visit our Web site at http://www.worldbook.com, or call 1-800-WORLDBK (967-5325).**

**For information about sales to schools and libraries, call 1-800-975-3250 (United States); 1-800-837-5365 (Canada).**



World Book, Inc.
233 N. Michigan Avenue
Chicago, IL 60601
U.S.A.

**Library of Congress Cataloging-in-Publication Data**

Monarchs and other butterflies.
p. cm. -- (World Book's animals of the world)
Includes bibliographical references and index.
ISBN 0-7166-1271-2 – ISBN 0-7166-1261-5
1. Monarch butterfly--Juvenile literature.
2. Butterflies--Juvenile literature. I. World Book, Inc.
II. Series.

QL561.D3M663 2005
595.78'9--dc22

2004016492

Printed in Malaysia
1 2 3 4 5 6 7 8 09 08 07 06 05

**Picture Acknowledgments:** Cover: © John Gerlach, Tom Stack & Associates; © David Kjaer, Nature Picture Library; © M. Sharp, Photo Researchers; © Scott W. Smith, Animals Animals; © Kim Taylor/Bob Stovall, Bruce Coleman Inc.

© Steve Austin, Papilio/Corbis 33; © Bill Beatty, Animals Animals 29; © Ruth Cole, Animals Animals 61; © Ray Coleman, Photo Researchers 39, 57; © Richard Cummins, Corbis 3, 7; © E. R. Degginger, Photo Researchers 37; © Michael Fogden, Animals Animals 21; © Michael & Patricia Fogden, Corbis 23; © Michael Gadomski, Photo Researchers 13; © Pam Gardner, Corbis 53; © John Gerlach, Tom Stack & Associates 43; © David Kjaer, Nature Picture Library 5, 55; © Dwight R. Kuhn 31; © Frans Lanting, Minden Pictures 19; © Danny Lehman, Corbis 11; © George Lepp, Corbis 15; © John Marechal, Bruce Coleman Inc. 5, 25, 27; © Brock May, Photo Researchers 59; © Hal Noss 51; © Joe Sartore, National Geographic Society/Getty Images 49; © David Schleser, Photo Researchers 47; © M. Sharp, Photo Researchers 41; © Scott W. Smith, Animals Animals 4, 35; © Alvin Staffan, Photo Researchers 45; © Kim Taylor/Bob Stovall, Bruce Coleman Inc. 8.

**Illustrations:** WORLD BOOK illustrations by John Fleck 17, 18, 20.

World Book's Animals of the World

# Monarchs

## and Other Butterflies

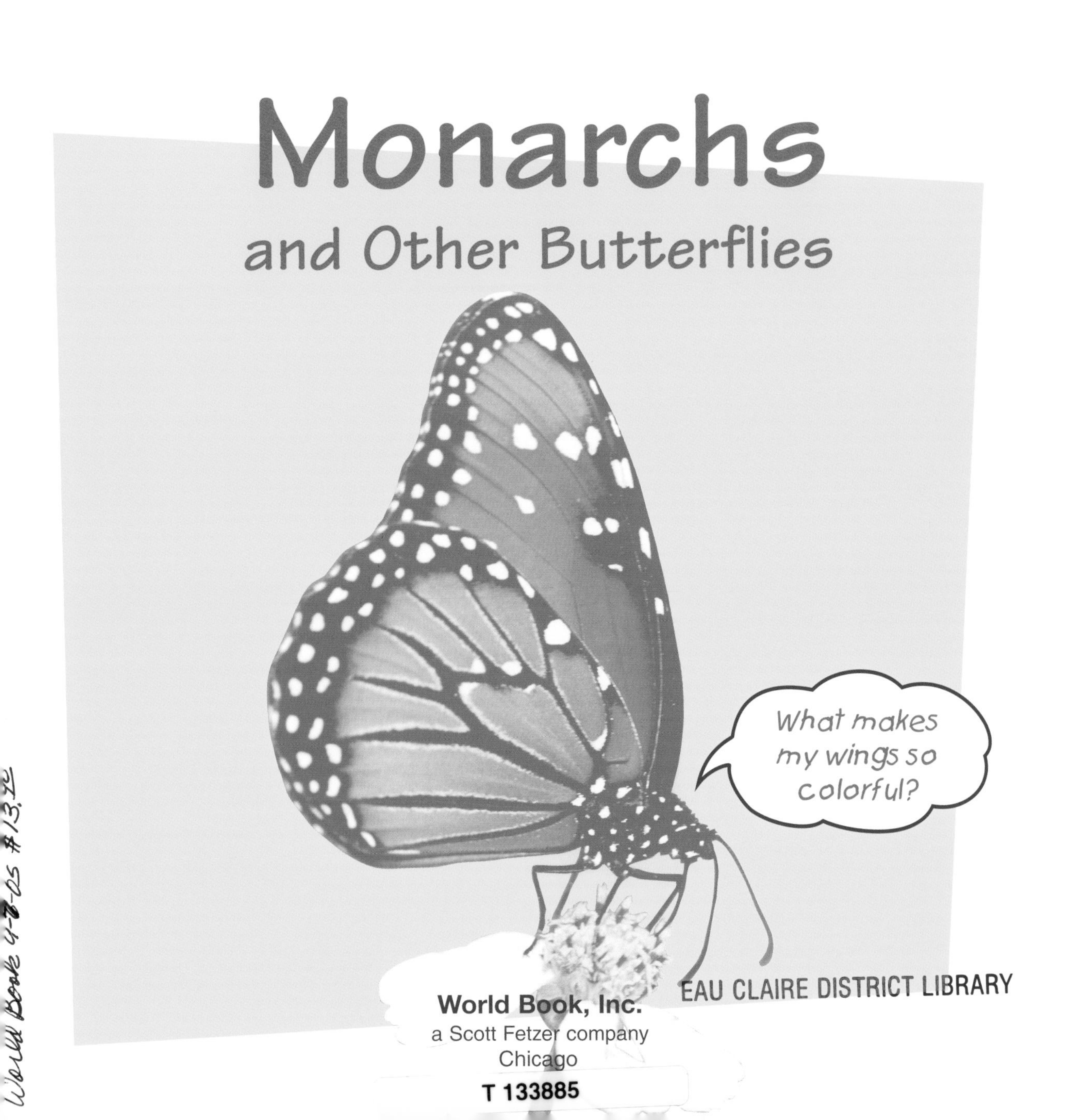




World Book, Inc.
a Scott Fetzer company
Chicago

# Contents

All I do is hang
around and wait!

Am I just a myth?

# What Is a Butterfly?

A butterfly is an insect. Insects are six-legged animals that have hard shells, or exoskeletons, on the outside of their bodies, instead of skeletons made of bones inside their bodies. Bees, wasps, and flies are also insects. So are ants, beetles, and fleas.

Many kinds of insects, including butterflies, have wings. They also have antennae on their heads. Antennae are sense organs. A butterfly uses its antennae to smell and to keep its balance.

Compared with most other insects, a butterfly has huge wings and a skinny body. In fact, it is hard to see a butterfly's body unless you look closely. One kind of butterfly is the large, orange butterfly called the monarch.

Butterflies have close relatives called moths. Scientists classify butterflies and moths together within a group of insects called Lepidoptera *(LEHP uh DOP tuhr uh).* This word means "scaly wings." Butterfly and moth wings are covered with thousands of tiny scales. Other insect wings do not have these tiny scales.

Monarch butterfly

# Where in the World Do Monarchs and Other Butterflies Live?

Butterflies live all around the world. They depend on plants for food, so they cannot live in frozen Antarctica. But, butterflies can be found on all other continents and on most islands.

Hundreds of years ago, monarch butterflies lived only in North America and South America. Over time, however, monarchs spread across the Pacific Ocean to Hawaii, New Zealand, Australia, and Indonesia. They also spread across the Atlantic Ocean to the Canary Islands and parts of Europe.

How might monarchs have spread around the world? They could have "hitched" rides on the many ships that travel back and forth between continents. Once in their new homes, the female butterflies might have laid eggs. Then, over time, the population of these newly transplanted insects could increase greatly.

Monarch butterfly

# Where Do Monarchs Spend the Winter?

In warm areas, such as Texas and Florida in the United States, monarchs can live the year round. But monarchs that live in other parts of North America migrate *(MY grayt)*, or travel, to places that stay fairly warm in winter.

Monarchs migrate up to 2,000 miles (3,200 kilometers) before winter starts. They set out flying from as far north as Canada in late summer. By late fall, they come to rest in California or Mexico. In those warm places, they form huge colonies. Some winters, as many as 100 million monarchs gather in colonies in Mexico.

No one knows for sure how monarchs find their way when they migrate. Perhaps they check the angle of the sun as they fly.

Monarchs cover a tree in their winter home

# How Do Other Butterflies Live Through Cold Winters?

Some butterflies hibernate *(HY buhr nayt)* during cold winter weather. The mourning cloak is one such butterfly.

In the fall, when the days are getting cool, the mourning cloak searches for a sheltered place. It snuggles into a pile of leaves under a log, a small crack in a brick wall, or some other cozy spot. Then the butterfly makes a special chemical in its body that keeps its blood from freezing.

When the days grow warmer in spring, the mourning cloak wakes up and begins to shiver. Shivering produces heat inside the butterfly's body. Soon, the mourning cloak is ready to fly away.

Many other kinds of butterflies hibernate, as well. Like the mourning cloak, they wake up as winter turns to spring.

Mourning cloak

# What Makes a Monarch's Wings So Colorful?

A monarch's wings are made up of thousands of tiny, thin, flat scales. Each scale has its own special color. The scales fit together to form a beautiful, complex pattern.

Other butterflies' wings are made of scales, too. And, so are moths' wings. No other type of insect has wing scales like those of butterflies and moths.

That is why the wings of flies, bees, and other insects are clear or much less colorful.

What colors can butterfly wings be? They can be black, white, gray, brown, tan, red, orange, and yellow. They also can be bright shades of blue, purple, and green.

A close view of a monarch's wing scales

# What Are the Parts of a Butterfly?

A butterfly has a thin body that might go unnoticed beside its big wings. Like the bodies of other animals, a butterfly body has a brain, stomach, heart, and other organs. And, as in other insects, the body parts of a butterfly are contained in three main regions—the head, thorax *(THAWR aks)*, and abdomen.

On its head, a butterfly has two eyes, two antennae, and a mouth, called the proboscis *(proh BOS ihs)*. The proboscis is a long, curled-up tube. When the butterfly sips nectar—a sweet liquid in flowers—the insect unrolls its proboscis and uses it like a straw.

The butterfly's legs and wings are attached to the thorax, the middle part of its body. Every butterfly has a pair of front and a pair of back wings. The back pair is partly tucked underneath the front pair.

The abdomen, or hind part of a butterfly's body, has holes called spiracles *(SPY ruh kulz)*. The butterfly breathes through the spiracles. The abdomen also contains reproductive and digestive organs.

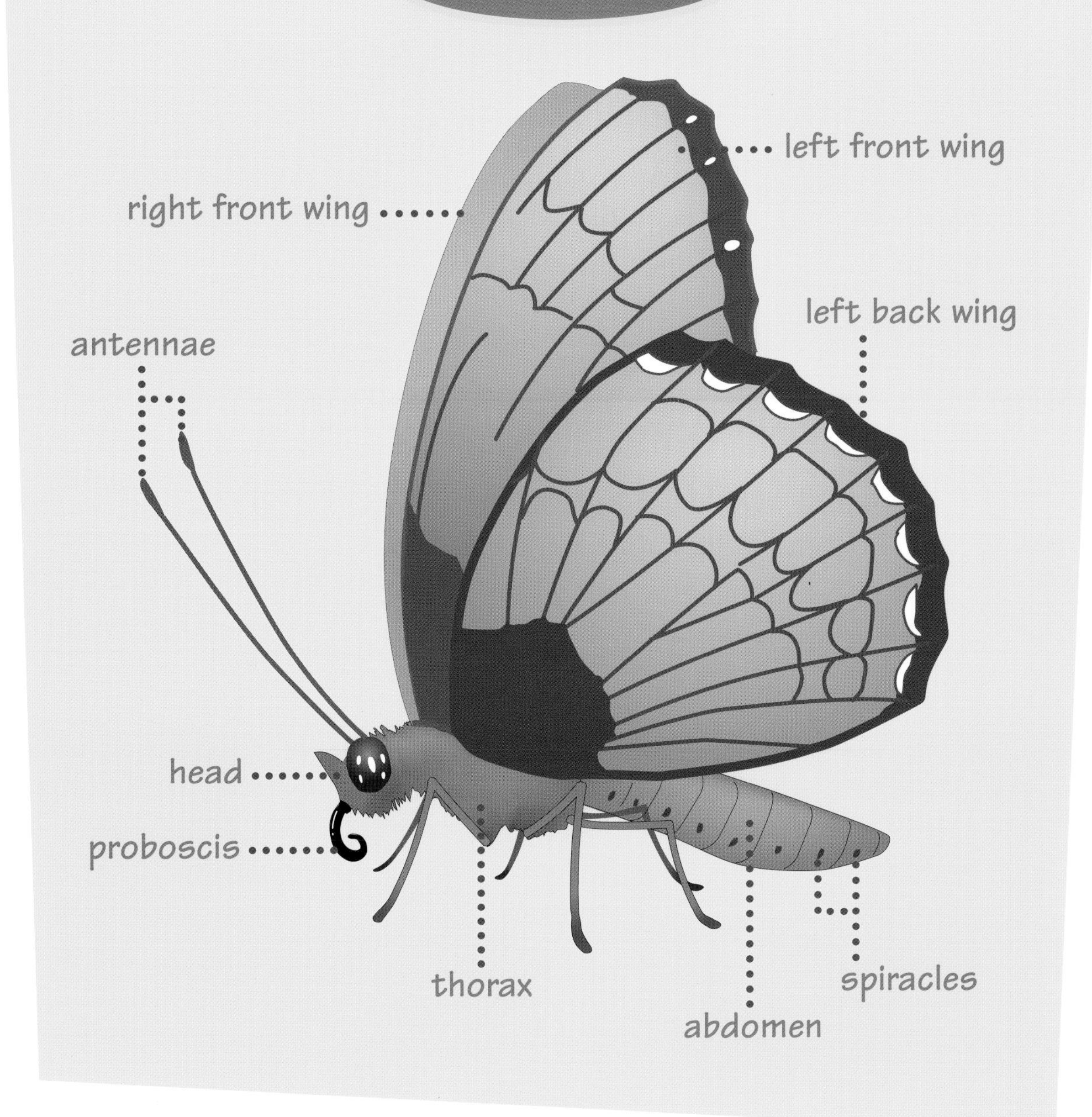
Diagram of a Butterfly
left front wing
right front wing
left back wing
antennae
head
proboscis
thorax
abdomen
spiracles

# How Are Butterflies Different from Moths?

Both butterflies and moths generally have wings that look large for their body size. Many of these insects have colorful designs on their wings.

There are, however, some important differences. Most butterflies fly in daylight, when their colors can be clearly seen. Moths fly mainly when it is dark.

A butterfly body is usually skinny and smooth. But, a moth body is thick and furry. Up close, an antenna of a butterfly is long and thin with a rounded tip. A moth antenna doesn't have a rounded tip—many moths have antennae that look a bit like feathers.

Butterflies and moths look different when they are resting from flight. A butterfly holds its wings upright. A moth holds its wings out flat or folded close to its body.

Two colorful Uranus moths with butterflies

# What Happens as a Butterfly Grows?

A butterfly goes through four stages during its life cycle. It spends the first stage developing within an egg. Then, the egg hatches and releases a hungry caterpillar and the second stage begins.

After a time, the caterpillar grows large from eating plants all the time. When fully grown, the caterpillar transforms into a pupa *(PYOO puh)*, which is the third stage. The pupa forms a shell around itself. This shell is called a chrysalis *(KRIHS uh lihs)*. Inside the chrysalis, the pupa changes and grows. In time, it breaks out of the shell as a butterfly!

The grown butterfly is in its fourth stage of life. Most adult butterflies live only one to two weeks. During that time, they lay eggs. Then the four stages of life start all over again.

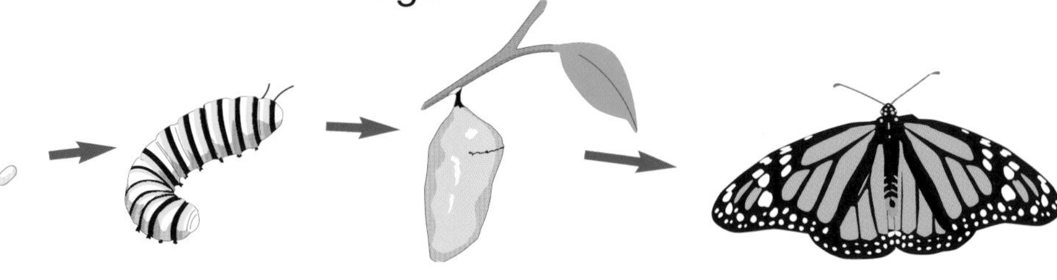

Pierid butterfly
laying eggs

# Why Does a Caterpillar Eat All the Time?

A caterpillar's first day starts when it hatches out of its egg. Right away the hungry animal eats its own eggshell. Then it searches for green plants to eat. But, chances are it won't need to search for long, because its mother probably laid her eggs near a good source of food.

The caterpillar starts eating and never stops. That's its job—to eat and eat. It is storing up energy to use in the next stages of its life.

With all its eating, the caterpillar soon becomes too big for its own skin. Then the caterpillar molts. That means its skin splits wide open. The caterpillar sheds its old skin like taking off a coat. (It had already formed a new skin beneath the skin it molted.) A caterpillar will molt several times as it grows.

Monarch caterpillar eating milkweed

# What Happens Inside a Chrysalis?

Many people think that butterflies emerge from silky cocoons. This, however, is rarely the case. Only moths and a few species of butterfly do that. Most butterflies develop within a chrysalis.

When a caterpillar has finished eating and growing, it is time to form a chrysalis. First, the caterpillar finds a sheltered spot where it deposits a silky substance from which it will hang. Then the caterpillar molts one more time to become a pupa. Soon, the outer shell of the pupa hardens and the chrysalis is complete.

If someone found a chrysalis on a branch or stem, he or she might think the animal inside was dead. Nothing could be further from the truth. The caterpillar is very busy. It is turning into a butterfly.

This entire process is called metamorphosis *(MEHT uh MAWR fuh sihs)*. The photos on pages 25 and 27 show some of the stages of this process of change.

1. Caterpillar after final molt
2. Pupa shell partially hardened
3. Chrysalis
4. Wings are visible inside chrysalis

# Is It Magic?

The alteration a pupa undergoes may seem magical, but, of course, no magic is involved. Scientists are able to explain the changes that happen within a chrysalis.

Researchers have found that certain chemicals produced by the pupa actually break down many of the pupa's body structures. This material is recycled and used to develop the new body parts needed by the adult butterfly.

When development is complete, the grown-up butterfly begins to separate itself from its chrysalis. The butterfly works hard to free itself. Out of the dead-looking chrysalis comes a beautiful butterfly!

The new butterfly has important work to do. It uses its front legs to "zip up" its proboscis, which was in two parts when the butterfly emerged. And, the insect pumps its folded-up wings full of air and blood, allowing them to spread out wide and to dry. Now the butterfly can take off.

Butterfly emerges
from chrysalis

# Can Butterflies See, Smell, Hear, Touch, and Taste?

Butterflies have sense organs, but they are not the same as human sense organs. If you looked at a butterfly's head close up, you would see two huge eyes. Butterflies, and many other insects, have compound eyes. That means that each eye is made up of many tiny lenses that form a honeycomb pattern. Scientists think that this type of eye is very good for seeing movement—an important ability for butterflies, which have many predators.

One of a butterfly's most important sense organs is made up of the two antennae on top of its head. They help a butterfly smell and balance and may help the butterfly hear and touch things, as well.

Which body part does a butterfly use to taste food? Although it seems unlikely, the answer is its feet. A butterfly's feet have tiny parts called cells that can taste. If a butterfly lands on a flower full of nectar, the cells signal the insect to start sipping.

Orange sulfur butterfly on a flower

# How Do Monarchs Protect Themselves?

To birds, frogs, spiders, and other animals who eat insects, a butterfly looks like dinner.

The monarch, however, protects itself by tasting bad to predators. When a bird takes a bite out of a monarch, the bird gets sick. Birds remember the bright pattern of a monarch's wing. A bird that gets sick from tasting one monarch probably won't try to eat another.

Monarch butterflies taste bad because monarch caterpillars eat milkweed plants. For most creatures, eating milkweed results in vomiting or even death. Protective chemicals that the caterpillar obtains by eating the milkweed remain with it through its metamorphosis into a butterfly. The bitter or poisonous juices of the milkweed plant are stored in the adult monarch's tissues, making the insect taste bad.

Viceroy butterflies have wings that look like monarch wings. Viceroys aren't the least bit poisonous. But birds think they are distasteful monarchs, and so they stay away.

Viceroy (left) and monarch (right)

# Do Some Butterflies Have Brushes for Legs?

Members of the brush-footed butterfly family have a pair of short, hairy front legs that look like brushes. These legs are not used for walking. Some scientists think the "brushes" on these front legs help the butterflies taste and smell things.

Brush-footed butterflies live in most parts of the world and include many butterflies that are common to North America. The viceroy is a brush-footed butterfly. So are the mourning cloak and the red admiral. Some scientists classify the monarch into this family as well, but others separate the monarch and its relatives into their own family—the milkweed butterflies.

Red admiral butterfly

# What Are Blues, Coppers, and Hairstreaks?

Blues, coppers, and hairstreaks make up a group of related butterflies that live all over the world. Most of these butterflies are rather small.

Most blues have bluish color somewhere on their wings. Coppers have copper color, which is reddish-brown, like a penny. Hairstreaks have "tails," called hairstreaks, on the lower end of their back wings.

The American copper is a common butterfly of North America. Another North American butterfly is the great purple hairstreak. The upper side of its wings are blue or purplish-blue. Each of its lower pair of wings ends in two hairstreaks; often, one is long and one short.

American copper butterfly

# What Are Sulfurs and Whites?

Sulfurs—sometimes spelled sulphurs—and whites make up a family of butterflies that live all over the world. Most of these butterflies, however, live in tropical lands.

In North America, including most of the United States, the orange sulfur is common. The upper side of its wings is yellow, but the lower side of the wings is often yellow-orange with dark outer edges. This butterfly is also called the alfalfa butterfly because the females lay their eggs on alfalfa. The orange sulfur caterpillar eats alfalfa plants.

Another common butterfly of this group is the cabbage white. It is a small white butterfly with tiny black spots and black tips on its upper wings. The caterpillar of the cabbage white eats cabbage and other leafy vegetables. Farmers and gardeners consider it a pest.

Orange sulfur butterfly

# Can Butterfly Wings Look Like Shiny Metal?

The answer is yes!

Metalmarks are a group of related butterflies that live all over the world. Many of them live in South America, but some live in North America. Most metalmark butterflies have bars or spots on their wings that look like silver or steel. That is why these butterflies are called metalmarks.

The little metalmark is a common butterfly in eastern North America. Another North American metalmark is the swamp metalmark. It is found in swamps in the northern United States. The swamp metalmark looks rather like the little metalmark, but its color is a bit brighter.

Swamp metalmark

# Can Butterflies Have Tails?

Each of the swallowtail butterfly's back wings comes to a long, skinny point. To many people, these points look like tails. But they are not real tails like those on cats or dogs.

Swallowtails all over the world are closely related. Most live in tropical places, although some familiar, beautiful kinds live in the United States.

Many swallowtails are large compared with other butterflies. Some of the largest kinds have wings that are nearly 10 inches (25 centimeters) across!

The tiger swallowtail is one of the largest and most beautiful butterflies. This butterfly has yellow wings striped in black in a pattern like that of a tiger's coat. When a tiger swallowtail opens its wings, it is more than 6 inches (15 centimeters) across.

Tiger swallowtail

# What Are Satyrs and Wood Nymphs?

Satyrs *(SAT uhrz)* and wood nymphs *(nihmfz)* are a group of related butterflies that live all over the world. The northern and southern pearly eye are examples of common satyrs in the United States. They are brown with eyespot markings near the edges of their wings.

Some scientists classify satyrs and wood nymphs in their own family. But other scientists include them into the brush-footed butterfly family.

Most kinds of satyrs and wood nymphs live in or near woods. They often perch on tree trunks. Most of these butterflies feed on flower nectar. But some sip sap from trees or liquids from rotting fruit or carrion (decaying meat).

Although most of these butterflies live in or near the woods, some are able to survive where it is too cold for trees to grow. These butterflies are sometimes called arctic butterflies. They can survive in the frozen tundra of the Arctic Circle or high up in the mountains.

Northern pearly
eye butterfly

# Do Some Butterflies Have Snouts?

Picture a fox or a dog. Each of these animals has a nose and mouth that sticks out from the head. This pointed part of the head is called a snout.

A small family of butterflies, called snout butterflies, has mouthparts that are long and snoutlike. But a snout butterfly does not have a true snout like a fox or a dog. A butterfly's snoutlike mouthparts seem to be used for camouflage. When the butterfly rests, these mouthparts look like the stalk of a leaf. So, the snout helps the butterfly disguise itself as a leaf and fool its predators.

Most snout butterflies live in tropical lands. One of the most common, the American snout butterfly—often simply called the snout butterfly—lives in a range that spans from Paraguay in South America to the southern United States.

Snout butterfly

# Are Skippers Butterflies?

Skippers are not true butterflies, but they are closely related to them and to moths. In fact, it can be hard to tell them apart.

But, looking closely at a skipper's antennae will help you identify these creatures. Most skippers have very characteristic hooks at the tips of their antennae. Butterflies have antennae with rounded or clubbed tips. Moth antennae are usually feathered.

Another way to identify a skipper is to watch it fly. A skipper darts and skips as it moves from one flower to another.

Skippers live in most parts of the world. About 300 species, or kinds, live in North America. Some of the skippers of North America include the checkered skipper, fiery skipper, Juvenal's duskywing, least skipperling, roadside skipper, and the silver-spotted skipper.

Silver-spotted skipper

# Do Butterflies Live in South America?

South America is home to thousands of kinds of butterflies. The steamy rain forests near the Amazon River provide good homes for them.

One of the biggest, brightest blue butterflies in the world lives in South America. It is the blue morpho butterfly. When the blue morpho opens its wings, they may be over 5 inches (about 13 centimeters) across. The blue morpho lives in rain forests from Venezuela to Brazil.

Another beautiful South American butterfly is the esmeralda. The wings of this butterfly are almost completely transparent, like glass. Only on the bottom edge of the back pair of wings is there any color. Bunches of scales in those places make small splashes of pink.

The 88 butterfly of South America is quite unusual. It has markings on the underside of its wings that clearly form a number. Guess what the number is!

Blue morpho butterfly

# Do Butterflies Live in Africa?

Of course they do! Africa has some of the world's most unusual and beautiful butterflies. The best homes for many kinds of butterflies are the jungles in western and central Africa.

Some of the world's reddest butterflies live in Africa. These red butterflies, known as the Cymothoes *(sye MOE thoez)*, live mainly in the rain forests of central Africa. Perhaps the brightest of these butterflies is the red glider.

The jungles of central Africa also are home to one of the world's largest butterflies. It is the African giant swallowtail. This huge swallowtail has very large upper wings. The span of an African giant swallowtail's wings can be as much as 10 inches (25 centimeters) across.

African giant
swallowtail butterfly

# Do Butterflies Live in Australia?

Yes, many butterflies live in wetter regions in northern and eastern Australia. Much of the land in middle and western Australia is desert. Few butterflies live in these very dry areas.

A close relative of North America's monarch butterfly lives in northern and eastern Australia. It is called the common crow. Like the monarch, this butterfly lays its eggs on milkweed plants. Also like the monarch, the caterpillar of this butterfly eats milkweed.

One of Australia's biggest and most colorful butterflies is the Cairns birdwing. This butterfly has a long, yellow body and big, richly colored wings. The wings of the female, when open, may stretch 5 inches (13 centimeters) across.

Cairns birdwing butterfly

# Do Butterflies Live in Europe?

Many kinds of butterflies live in Europe. European countries have some of the same kinds of butterflies as those found in North America. The painted lady, cabbage white, and red admiral live in both Europe and North America. Europe also has skippers, wood nymphs, and swallowtails that are very similar to those found in North America.

One of the most unusual butterflies of Europe is the peacock. This butterfly has four huge eyespots, one on each wing. The eyespots frighten predators when the butterfly opens its wings.

An especially beautiful European butterfly is the Adonis blue. It is common in England and also lives throughout continental Europe. The male of this butterfly has brilliant blue wings with crisp, white edges on its upper side. The females are brown. The butterfly is named for Adonis, a beautiful young man from a myth told in Ancient Greece.

Adonis blue butterfly

# Do Butterflies Live in Asia?

Butterflies live in most parts of Asia. In the tropical lands of Southeast Asia, there are many kinds of butterflies.

Southeast Asia is home to large, colorful swallowtails. Many of these swallowtails have skinny back wings with uneven edges. This type of lower wing is sometimes called a "clubtail."

The orange albatross is another attractive butterfly found in Southeast Asia. This butterfly's wings are almost solid orange.

The Japanese emperor butterfly is the national butterfly of Japan. Its wings are mostly purplish-blue with many small white spots and a pink spot at the tip of each back wing. This beautiful butterfly also lives in China.

Japanese emperor butterfly

# What Is a Butterfly Garden?

A butterfly garden, of course, is a garden designed to attract butterflies!

To attract swallowtails, a butterfly garden should include herbs from the parsley family. Swallowtails lay their eggs on these plants. Even plants that are usually considered "weeds" might be good to have in a butterfly garden. Of course, to entice monarchs to lay their eggs in a butterfly garden, milkweed must be chosen.

Brightly colored blossoms draw butterflies to nectar in the flowers. Butterflies especially like red, orange, yellow, and purple. To attract feeding adult butterflies, butterfly gardens should include plants that have flowers of these colors.

A butterfly garden should be a safe place for the insects. Strong chemicals called insecticides *(ihn SEHK tuh sydz)* should not be used. These chemicals kill harmful insects. But they kill butterflies, too.

Butterfly garden

# Are Butterflies in Danger?

Some species, or kinds, of butterflies are in danger of becoming extinct. In many places in the world the number of butterflies is dropping.

Worldwide, there are over 40 species (types) of butterflies, skippers, and moths that are considered to be endangered or that are in danger of extinction. Little is known about the status of hundreds more species.

The Karner blue butterfly is one example of an endangered butterfly. In the past, the Karner blue lived in many places in the northern United States. But farms, highways, and houses have taken over most of the land on which Karner blues used to live.

In addition to habitat loss, butterflies in many places live in danger of being poisoned. People use pesticides to kill harmful insects. These chemicals also kill butterflies, bees, and other helpful insects.

One way to help butterflies is to plant butterfly gardens and to learn about the species that appear in those gardens.

Karner blue butterfly

# Butterfly Fun Facts

- The world's largest butterfly is from Papua New Guinea. The wingspread of the Queen Alexandra's birdwing is 11 inches (28 centimeters) across.
- Monarch caterpillars eat only milkweed plants. If a monarch butterfly chooses to lay her eggs on the wrong kind of plant, her caterpillars will starve to death.
- Airplane pilots have seen monarchs flying more than 10,000 feet (some 3,000 meters) above the ground.
- The word *butterfly* comes from an old English word meaning "butter-colored flying creature." Because yellow butterflies were common in England, this name evolved into the English word for all of these insects.
- Some male butterflies carry "love dust" on their wings. The dust contains chemicals that attract females. A male brushes some of the love dust onto a female he wants to court.

# Glossary

**abdomen** The hind part of an insect's body.

**camouflage** Features of an animal, such as its color, that help it blend into its surroundings.

**carrion** Dead, decaying animal flesh.

**caterpillar** The young, wormlike stage in the life cycle of a butterfly or moth.

**chrysalis** The third stage in the development of a butterfly; adult butterfly features develop inside a chrysalis.

**compound eye** An eye made up of many tiny lenses.

**egg** The first stage in the development of a butterfly; a caterpillar hatches from the egg.

**endangered** In danger of extinction, or dying out.

**exoskeleton** The hard, outer covering that protects the body of such animals as insects.

**eyespots** Spots on the wings of certain insects that resemble large eyes.

**hibernate** To sleep through the cold months.

**larva** The second stage in the development of a butterfly; the caterpillar is a butterfly larva.

**metamorphosis** The process in which a caterpillar changes into an adult butterfly or moth.

**migrate** To travel from one region to another because of a change in the season.

**molt** To shed old shell, skin, feathers, or other body coverings.

**nectar** The sugary liquid inside flowers that butterflies eat.

**proboscis** The sucking, tubelike mouthpart of butterflies and certain other insects.

**pupa** The inactive stage of an insect's life cycle during which the young changes into an adult.

**thorax** The middle part of an insect's body.

# Index

(**Boldface** indicates a photo or illustration.)



**For more information about Monarchs and Other Butterflies, try these resources:**


*Butterflies and Moths,* by Elaine Pascoe, Blackbirch Press, 1997.

*Eyewitness Explorers: Butterflies and Moths,* by John Feltwell, Dorling Kindersley, 1993.

*An Extraordinary Life: The Story of a Monarch Butterfly,* by Laurence P. Pringle, Orchard Books, 1997.

http://www.mesc.usgs.gov/resources/education/butterfly/bfly_intro.asp

http://www.monarchwatch.org/

http://www.npwrc.usgs.gov/resource/distr/lepid/bflyusa/bflyusa.htm

# Insect Classification

Scientists classify animals by placing them into groups. The animal kingdom is a group that contains all the world's animals. Phylum, class, order, and family are smaller groups. Each phylum contains many classes. A class contains orders, an order contains families, and a family contains individual species. Each species also has its own scientific name. (The abbreviation "spp." after a genus name indicates that a group of species from a genus is being discussed.) Here is how the animals in this book fit into this system.

## Insects and their relatives (Phylum Arthropoda)

### Insects (Class Insecta)

#### Butterflies, moths, and skippers (Order Lepidoptera)

**Blues, coppers, hairstreaks, and their relatives (Family Lycaenidae)**

- Adonis blue ........ *Lysandra bellargus*
- American copper ........ *Lycaena phlaeas*
- Great purple hairstreak ........ *Atlides halesus*
- Karner blue ........ *Lycaeides melissa samuelis*

**Brush-footed butterflies (Family Nymphalidae)**

- 88 butterflys ........ *Diaethria* spp.
- Blue morphos ........ *Morpho* spp.
- Japanese emperor ........ *Sasakia charonda*
- Mourning cloak ........ *Nymphalis antiopa*
- Painted lady ........ *Vanessa cardui*
- Peacock ........ *Inachis io*
- Red admiral ........ *Vanessa atalanta*
- Red glider ........ *Cymothoe sangaris*
- Viceroy ........ *Limenitis archippus*

**Metalmarks (Family Riodinidae)**

- Little metalmark ........ *Calephelis virginiensis*
- Swamp metalmark ........ *Calephelis mutica*

**Milkweed butterflies (Family Danaidae)**

- Common crow ........ *Euploea core*
- Monarch ........ *Danaus plexippus*

**Satyrs, wood nymphs, and their relatives (Family Satyridae)**

- Arctic butterflies ........ *Erebia* spp.
- Esmeralda ........ *Cithaerias esmeralda*
- Northern pearly eye ........ *Enodia anthedon*
- Southern pearly eye ........ *Enodia portlandia*

**Skippers (Family Hesperiidae)**

- Common roadside skipper ........ *Amblyscirtes vialis*
- Common checkered skipper ........ *Pyrgus communis*
- Fiery skipper ........ *Hylephila phyleus*
- Juvenal's duskywing ........ *Erynnis juvenalis*
- Least skipperling ........ *Ancyloxypha numitor*
- Silver-spotted skipper ........ *Epargyreus clarus*

**Snout butterflies (Family Libytheidae)**

- American snout butterfly ........ *Libytheana carinenta*

**Sulfurs and whites (Family Pieridae)**

- Cabbage white ........ *Pieris rapae*
- Orange albatross ........ *Appias nero*
- Orange sulfur butterfly ........ *Colias eurytheme*

**Swallowtails and birdwings (Family Papilionidae)**

- African giant swallowtail ........ *Papilio antimachus*
- Cairns birdwing ........ *Ornithoptera priamus*
- Queen Alexandra's birdwing ........ *Ornithoptera alexandrae*
- Tiger swallowtail ........ *Papilio glaucus*

**Uranus moths (Family Uraniidae)**